Save the Birds

Fay Robinson
Illustrated by Neecy Twinem

Rigby®

"We have sandwiches for lunch!" said Nahee's father as he pulled food out of the bag.

The Cho family happily ate their lunch.

"I love spending the afternoon at this park!" exclaimed Nahee.

"I love coming to this park, too," said Dad. Elmwood Park was the only city park that had trees, a pond, and lots of birds. Dad stretched out on the blanket and looked up at the trees.

Nahee and her little sister Jinwon listened to Dad as they finished their lemonade.

"This park was much larger before those apartments were built," said Dad.

"Look at that bird!" called Nahee, sitting up suddenly. A bright red bird flew above them on its way to a tree.

"That's a cardinal," said Nahee's mom.

"Look! That bird on the nest might be the mother bird!" said Jinwon.

Looking around, Nahee and Jinwon saw bird nests in every tree. "Think about all of the baby birds that will be born soon!" said Nahee.

Nahee, Jinwon, and Dad rode their bikes to the park almost every day to look at the birds' nests. Nahee and Jinwon could hardly wait to see the baby birds after they were born.

But one day, when they got to the park, they saw workers putting up signs.

"What are those workers doing here, and what do the signs say?" asked Jinwon.

"They're closing the park next month, but the signs don't tell why!" said Nahee. Nahee saw a man in a suit telling people what to do.

"He looks like he's the boss," Nahee said, tugging on Dad's arm, "so let's go and talk to him."

Dad walked over to the man and asked, "Why is the park closing?"

"We're going to chop down all of these trees so that we can build a shopping center here," said the man.

"But what about the birds?" asked Nahee.

"The birds will just fly away, so you don't need to worry about them," said the man.

"But the birds have made nests in these trees!" said Nahee. "What will happen to their eggs?" She pointed to a red cardinal as it flew past on its way to a nest.

"That is a beautiful bird," said the man as he watched the cardinal. "I'll have to think about that."

Dad walked away slowly, and the girls followed him, thinking about what might happen to the birds.

"How many birds will lose their nests if they cut down all of the trees?" asked Nahee.

"Well, about how many trees are there?" asked Dad.

Nahee ran from tree to tree, slapping her hand against each one as she counted.

When she got to 20, Dad
said, "That's enough. Now we
can estimate. You counted about
one-fifth of the trees. If we multiply the
20 trees you counted by 5, we get 100.
So there are about 100 trees altogether."

"About how many nests do you think
are in the trees?" asked Dad.

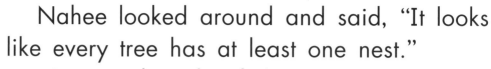

Nahee looked around and said, "It looks like every tree has at least one nest."

"So," said Dad, "if there are 100 trees, that would be at least 100 nests."

"That means that 100 or more nests will be lost!" said Nahee.

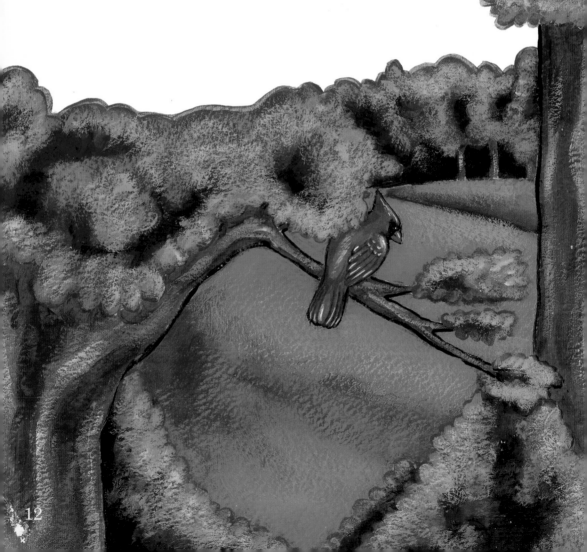

After she got home, Nahee continued talking about the birds and the workers.

"Since you're so concerned about what they're planning to do, maybe you should let people know," suggested Mom.

"Yes, let the builders know that you oppose their plan," added Dad. "If you get a large group of people to agree with you, the builders might listen. I'm sure that some of the other families who enjoy the park will feel the same way."

Nahee, Dad, Mom, and Jinwon decided to make signs, using cardboard and long sticks, so that everyone would know how they felt.

The next day, Nahee and her family loaded the signs into the car and went to the park. People in the park stopped to ask them about their signs.

"They're going to cut down all of the trees, and all of these beautiful birds will lose their nests," explained Nahee. "And just think about how many eggs are in all those nests!"

Just as Nahee had hoped, many families wanted to hold signs, too. Many more people stopped to ask questions about the park and the birds.

They walked back and forth through the park all afternoon. Together all of the people sang,

Save the park! Save the trees!
Save the birds! Save them, please!

"Now what happens?" asked Nahee as she helped put the signs back into the car.

"Now we wait to see if any of the people building the shopping center were listening," replied Dad.

Nahee and Jinwon went to the park with Mom or Dad every day to see if anything had changed. The workers' signs were still up, but the trees hadn't been cut down yet either.

Then one day Mom shouted, "Everyone, come and see what's in the newspaper!" She began reading to them. "Plans to turn Elmwood Park into a shopping center have been stopped. Last week more than 25 people carried signs in the park, opposing the plan. Mr. Johnson, one of the builders, said that the people carrying the signs made him realize that many birds would lose their nests if he cut down the trees. He now plans to build the shopping center down the street where there are no trees to cut down."

"We saved the birds, didn't we?" asked Nahee.

"We sure did!" exclaimed Dad.

"Let's go to the park," said Mom excitedly.

"I'll make sandwiches!" said Jinwon.

When they got to the park, Nahee ran straight to a tree with a bird's nest. "Look at the baby cardinals!" she said, pointing up at the nest.

Four little birds were moving their heads. The mother bird carefully placed some food into each bird's mouth, while the father bird brought more.

"I'm hungry like the baby birds," said Nahee, pulling out the sandwiches. "Jinwon, there are only three sandwiches in the bag!"

"Well, I estimated just like we did with the trees," said Jinwon.

"Estimating is a good way to figure out how many birds there are in a park, but it's not very good when you're making sandwiches for the four of us!" said Mom as she smiled. "When you know the exact number, you don't need to estimate."

"Jinwon, we can share this one," said Dad as he cut the sandwich in half.

Nahee, Jinwon, Mom, and Dad enjoyed eating their sandwiches and sitting in the shade of the trees. But most of all, they liked watching the baby birds in the trees, enjoying their first meals.

Suddenly Nahee began to sing quietly,
We saved the birds!
We saved their nests!
We saved the park!
We are the best!